ARCHIVAL PRINCIPLES FOR CHURCHES

An illustrated guide for beginning and maintaining congregational archives

Foreword by Wm. R. Estep

by
JEANETTE WHITE FORD

Wipf and Stock Publishers
EUGENE, OREGON

Wipf and Stock Publishers
199 West 8th Avenue, Suite 3
Eugene, Oregon 97401

Archival Principles of Churches
An Illustrated Guide for Beginning and Maintaining Congregational Archives
By Ford, Jeanette White
Copyright©2002 Ford, Jeanette White
ISBN: 1-59244-088-6
Publication Date: November, 2002

Foreword

Every church needs archives. The question immediately arises: What are archives anyway? Even those who can answer this question without difficulty may wonder why any church would need them. This is because the term generally conjures up buildings with miles of shelves loaded with books and papers, all with their official stamps and seals.

Archivist Jeanette Ford has something similar but also quite different in mind in this delightfully useful book. The large letters in which the text is printed coupled with the cartoon figures make concepts and archival principles, which for the uninitiated can be quite complex or even confusing, clear and easily understood. One wonders why any church should not have its own archives?

Most churches have laying around the premises in an unorganized and haphazard way, collections of papers and minute books, "the stuff" out of which archives are born. The author shows in this creatively written and illustrated work how it can be done. As a church historian, I know why it ought to be done.

Wm. R. Estep

Distinguished Professor of Church History,
Emeritus, Southwestern Baptist Theological
Seminary, Fort Worth, 1997

Contents

1. Why Do Churches Need Archives?   3
2. How Can Churches Begin Archives?   27
3. Which Records Should Be Kept?   51
4. How Should Archival Materials Be Organized?   75
5. How Can Archival Materials Be Preserved?   117
6. How Can Churches Use Archives?   131

Book Summary   142

Chapter I

WHY DO CHURCHES NEED ARCHIVES?

"YOU'VE RAISED A GOOD POINT."

"ARCHIVES ARE THE OFFICIAL, NON-CURRENT RECORDS OF A CHURCH WHICH HAVE BEEN PRESERVED FOR FUTURE USE."

"OFFICIAL?
I SUPPOSE YOU MEAN RECORDS WHICH ARE MADE BY CHURCH OFFICERS OR IN A CHURCH OFFICE.

BUT, NON-CURRENT? DOES THAT MEAN LIKE THINGS YOU WOULD FIND IN A MUSEUM?"

An ARCHIVES PROVIDES A CLEAR PICTURE OF A CHURCH'S PAST -- UNDISTORTED BY BIAS, PREJUDICE, OR FORGETFULNESS.

AN ARCHIVES HELPS A CHURCH TO REMEMBER ITS ORIGINAL PURPOSE.

GO,
TELL,
TEACH.

An ARCHIVES ALSO PRESERVES PERSONAL RECORDS WHICH REFLECT FAMILY HISTORY —— SUCH AS BAPTISMAL, MARRIAGE, AND DEATH RECORDS.

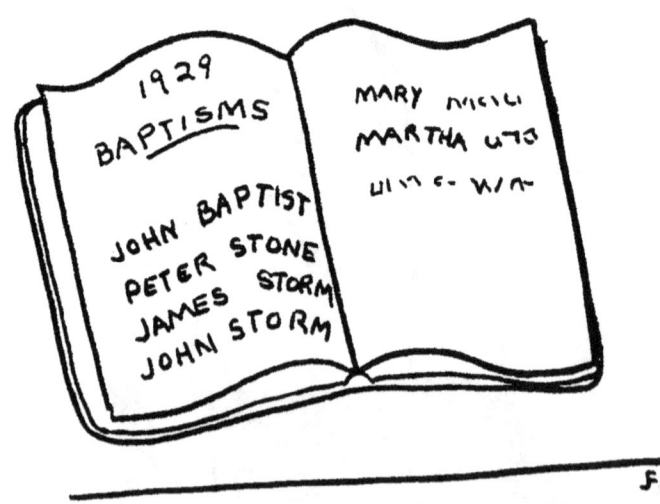

AN ARCHIVES DEMONSTRATES THE INFLUENCE OF THE CHURCH IN THE COMMUNITY.

AS WELL AS AVOID MISTAKES OF EARLIER YEARS.

1972
STAND UP, SIT DOWN, LOOK AROUND FINANCIAL CAMPAIGN

ANNIVERSARIES AND OTHER CELEBRATIONS ARE ENHANCED BY A DISPLAY OF ARCHIVAL MATERIALS.

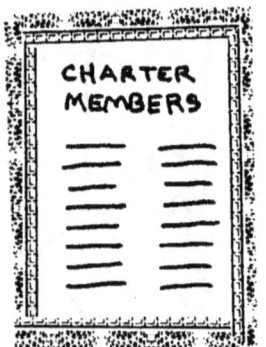

AND LAST, AN ARCHIVES MAKES THE **WRITING** OF CHURCH HISTORY MORE **COMPLETE** AND MORE **ACCURATE**.

LET'S REVIEW
CHAPTER I

Of the reasons given on pages 11 through 22, which do you think best answer the question, "Why do churches need archives?"

1._____

2._____

Fill in the blanks below to complete a definition of church archives.

"Church archives are the o_____, non-_____ records of a church which are p_____ for future use."

(upside down: official, current, preserved)

Chapter II

HOW CAN CHURCHES BEGIN ARCHIVES?

INERTIA
IS THE MAIN PROBLEM.

THESE FOUR PROCEDURES WILL HELP YOU GET

STARTED.

1. ENLIST AN ARCHIVIST AND STAFF.

2. LOCATE CHURCH'S HISTORICAL RECORDS.

3. DESIGNATE A STORAGE AREA.

4. PURCHASE SUPPLIES.

LET'S EXAMINE EACH OPERATION.

1. ENLIST
AN ARCHIVIST AND STAFF.

SOME CHURCHES CALL THIS A HISTORICAL COMMITTEE.

SOME QUALIFICATIONS
FOR THIS TASK ARE:

A LOVE OF
HISTORY,

THE ABILITY TO COMPLETE A TASK.

THE SECOND STEP IS:

2. LOCATE HISTORICAL RECORDS.

ASK THE PASTOR TO HELP PUBLICIZE THE SEARCH.

SECRETARIES

MAY HAVE

VALUABLE

SUGGESTIONS.

THE BUILDING CUSTODIAN COULD HELP LOCATE A TREASURE TROVE.

ADVERTIZE IN VARIOUS WAYS.

USE THE CHURCH BULLETIN TOO.

SET A **DEADLINE** FOR COLLECTION OF RECORDS.

THE THIRD PROCEDURE IS:

3. DESIGNATE A STORAGE SPACE,

NEAR A PROCESS & RESEARCH AREA,

TEMPERATURE AND HUMIDITY
CONTROLLED, IF POSSIBLE.

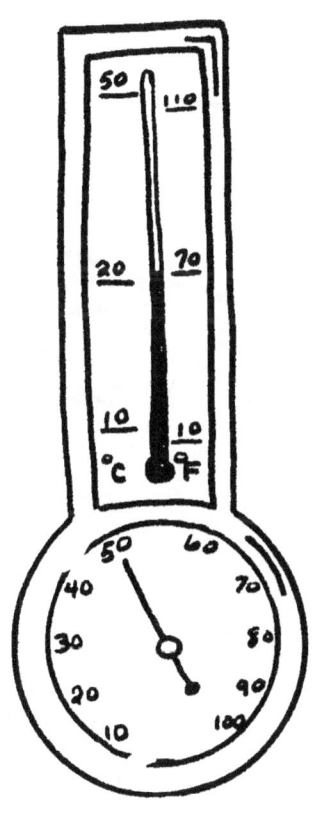

IN HOT OR COLD ATTICS,

45

IN A COFFEE BREAK ROOM,

THE LAST STEP IS:
4. PURCHASE SUPPLIES.

- ACID-FREE FILE FOLDERS

- ARCHIVES BOXES

- CUBIC FOOT CARTONS

- BAKED ENAMEL FILE CABINETS

- CHALK

- MARKING PENS

- LABELS

CHAPTER II
REVIEW

FOUR STEPS IN BEGINNING AN ARCHIVES ARE:

1. E_____ __ A_____
   __ _____.

2. L_____ __ R_____.

3. _____ _ S__ A__.

4. P_____ S_____.

1. Enlist an archivist and staff. 2. Locate church records. 3. Designate a storage area. 4. Purchase supplies.

Chapter III

WHICH RECORDS SHOULD BE PRESERVED?

NO! ALMOST ALL CHURCH RECORDS NEED WINNOWING...

TO SEPARATE THE WHEAT FROM THE CHAFF.

CONSIDER THIS,
CHURCH RECORDS ARE
CREATED TO FILL
AN ADMINISTRATIVE
NEED,

BUT...

TO HELP DETERMINE THE
WORTH
OF A RECORD, ASK THESE
QUESTIONS:

WHAT IS THE RECORD'S
LEGAL VALUE?
ARTISTIC VALUE?
HISTORIC VALUE?
FAMILY VALUE?
DENOMINATIONAL VALUE?
EMOTIONAL VALUE?
ADMINISTRATIVE VALUE?

ASK, IF THIS DOCUMENT WERE DATED 100 YEARS EARLIER, WOULD I FIND IT MORE INTERESTING, INFORMATIVE, WORTHWHILE?

REVIVAL EXPENSES
OCTOBER 1892

STAGE COACH TICKET $12.

BOARDING HOUSE 2 WEEKS $14.

LOVE OFFERING FOR EVANGELIST $22.50

LOVE OFFERING FOR SONG LEADER $12.

ASK,
IS THE DOCUMENT WELL PRESERVED?

IF RECORDS ARE ILLEGIBLE, MILDEWED, DAMAGED BY RODENTS OR INSECTS, THEY MAY NOT BE WORTH KEEPING.

THE KEY TO SIGNIFICANT QUALITY IN ARCHIVES IS RECORDS MANAGEMENT.

THIS MEANS A CHURCH SHOULD ADEQUATELY DOCUMENT ITS ACTIONS.

RECORDS MANAGEMENT ALSO MEANS THAT A CHURCH SHOULD DECIDE WHICH RECORDS TO

RETAIN PERMANENTLY.

BUT A **WRITTEN SELECTION GUIDE** IS A MORE **RELIABLE METHOD!**

RECORDS WHICH PROVIDE A GOOD PICTURE OF A CHURCH'S HISTORY ARE —

STAFF CORRESPONDENCE,

MINUTES of CHURCH BUSINESS MEETINGS,

WEEKLY BULLETINS,

AND
PHOTOGRAPHS
IDENTIFIED BY DATE, PLACE, PERSONS AND ACTIVITY.

SAMPLE
Church Records Selection Guide

I. Records Relating to the Origin and Development of the Church
   A. Incorporation documents.
   B. Constitution and by-laws with dated amendments.
   C. Records of earlier organizations.

II. Records Relating to Church Staff
   A. Licensing & Ordination records.
   B. Official correspondence, i.e. relating to church operations and not confidential or personal files.
   C. Job descriptions.
   D. Copies of calls to professional staff.
   E. Photographs of staff and families.

III. Records Relating to Membership
   A. Membership rolls.
   B. Records of christenings, baptisms, confirmations, marriages, deaths, etc.
   C. Cemetery records.
   D. Records of missionaries.

IV. Records Relating to Organization
   A. Copies of statistical and narrative reports to association, synod, or diocese.
   B. Annual lists of deacons, trustees, boards, officers and committees.
   C. Minutes of business meetings.
   D. Reports and recommendations of committees.
   E. Records of church organizations.
      1. Sunday School
      2. Church training
      3. Mission groups.
      4. Choirs.

V. Financial Records
   A. Annual budgets.
   B. Non-current treasurer's reports.
   C. Non-current receipt and disbursement ledgers.

VI. Property Records
   A. Blueprints and specifications.
   B. Construction contracts, etc.
   C. Mortgages and retired mortgages.
   D. Deeds, titles, etc.
   E. Property surveys, city/county permits, variances.
   F. Insurance contracts, damage reports.
   G. Interior and exterior photographs of buildings and furnishings.

VII. Published Records
   A. Bulletins and newsletters.
   B. Membership and pictorial directories.
   C. Histories of the church and/or its organizations.
   D. Programs for special events.
   E. Sermons, audiotapes, videotapes.
   F. Newspaper features or advertisements.

VIII. Miscellaneous Records
   A. Photographs.
      1. Organizations.
      2. Special events.
      3. Historical.
   B. Records about noted church members or special events.
   C. Museum pieces. (Available space and the value of artifacts will determine this collection. Normally, these items are not included in archives.)

SUMMARY 3

THE MOST RELIABLE METHOD FOR RETAINING CHURCH RECORDS IS A _____ _____ _____.

SELECTION OF RECORDS FOR ARCHIVES REQUIRES BOTH _____ AND _____ OF DOCUMENTS.

RECORDS YOUR CHURCH MAY DECIDE TO RETAIN MIGHT INCLUDE

_____
_____
_____
_____.

Records selection guide. preservation, disposal. Choose items from the sample records selection guide.

Chapter IV

HOW SHOULD ARCHIVAL MATERIALS BE ORGANIZED?

THE DIFFERENCE
BETWEEN A PILE OF
BROKEN GLASS...

AND A STAINED GLASS WINDOW IS ARRANGEMENT.

IN THE SAME MANNER, THE DIFFERENCE BETWEEN

A ROOMFUL OF DUSTY CHURCH RECORDS

AND AN ARCHIVES

IS

ARRANGEMENT.

RECORDS MUST NOT ONLY BE ARRANGED IN AN ORDERLY MANNER, THEY MUST ALSO BE

DESCRIBED TO AID A RESEACHER TO DETERMINE WHAT RECORDS ARE AVAILABLE.

SOMEONE MAY ASK,

"WHO WAS THE PASTOR IN 1957?"

OR ___

OR _ _

"WHAT WAS THE CHURCH BUDGET IN 1933?"

EFFICIENT ARRANGEMENT AND DESCRIPTION OF RECORDS PAVE THE WAY TO ANSWER SUCH QUESTIONS.

AS THE ARCHIVISTS ARRANGE RECORDS THEY CAN ALSO MAKE NOTES FOR USE IN WRITING DESCRIPTIONS.

CHURCH RECORDS

WILL PROBABLY NEED TO BE ARRANGED ON SEVERAL LEVELS.

1. RECORD GROUP.
2. SUB-GROUP.
3. SERIES.
4. FILE UNITS.

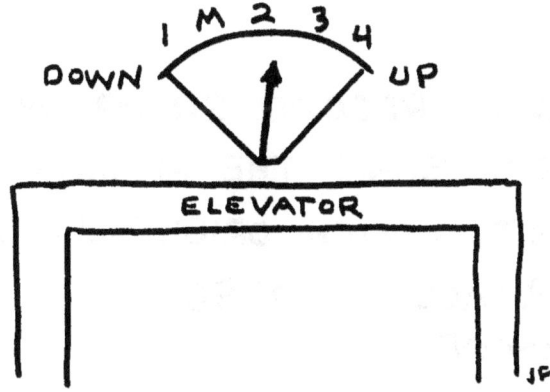

1. RECORD GROUP.

A CHURCH ARCHIVES SHOULD BE ORGANIZED BY RECORD GROUPS.

EACH RECORD GROUP WILL REPRESENT THE ADMINISTRATIVE UNIT WHICH ORIGINALLY MADE OR ACCUMULATED THE RECORDS.

THE FRENCH FIRST USED RECORD GROUPS AFTER THE REVOLUTION WHEN THEY TOOK CUSTODY OF THE ROYAL RECORDS.

THEY CALLED IT

RESPECT DES FONDS.

THIS MEANS THAT RECORDS FROM ONE SOURCE MUST NOT BE MINGLED WITH RECORDS FROM ANOTHER SOURCE.

2. SUB GROUP.

FOR MORE DEFINITIVE ORGANIZATION, RECORD GROUPS MAY BE DIVIDED INTO SUB GROUPS.*

* SMALLER GROUPS MAY NOT NEED TO BE SUBDIVIDED.

ANOTHER EXAMPLE:

RECORD GROUP
CHURCH PUBLISHED MATERIALS.

SUB GROUPS
- ✓ BULLETINS
- ✓ NEWS LETTERS
- ✓ MEMBERSHIP DIRECTORIES
- ✓ PROGRAMS FOR SPECIAL EVENTS
- ✓ CHURCH HISTORIES
- ✓ SERMONS
- ✓ ADVERTISEMENTS

3. SERIES.

THE BASIC UNIT OF AN ARCHIVAL COLLECTION IS A SERIES.

A SERIES IS A GROUP OF RECORDS RELATED TO EACH OTHER BY ___

SUBJECT,

4. FILE UNITS.

EACH SERIES OF RECORDS MAY BE ARRANGED INTERNALLY BY FILE UNITS.

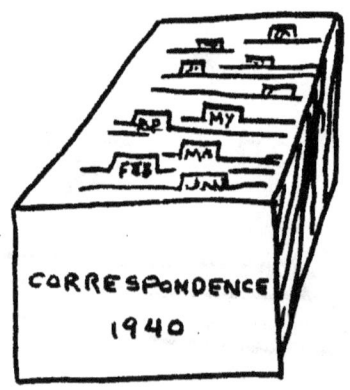

THIS CORRESPONDENCE SERIES IS ARRANGED
- CHRONOLOGICALLY IN FILE UNITS.

IF POSSIBLE, THE **ORIGINAL ORDER** OF RECORDS SHOULD BE **PRESERVED.**

THIS MEANS THE ARCHIVIST WILL ARRANGE DOCUMENTS IN THE SAME ORDER THAT THE CREATOR OF THE RECORDS ARRANGED THEM.

BUT, IF THE RECORDS ARE IN COMPLETE DISARRAY, THE ARCHIVIST MAY IMPOSE A SYSTEM OF ORGANIZATION TO AID RETRIEVAL.

IN THIS CASE, THE SIMPLEST SYSTEM IS THE BEST SYSTEM!

TODAY, OUR TOPIC IS "THE IMPORTANCE OF ORIGINAL ORDER." (WITH 3 POINTS AND A POEM.)

I. ORIGINAL ORDER PROTECTS THE <u>RELATIONSHIP</u> OF ONE RECORD TO ANOTHER.

II. ORIGINAL ORDER PROVIDES A WORKABLE AND ECONOMICAL <u>GUIDE</u> FOR ARRANGING RECORDS.

III. ORIGINAL ORDER PROCLAIMS THE <u>SIGNIFICANCE</u> OF THE RECORDS.

(WE PROMISED YOU A POEM.)

A LIMERICK ON THE PERILS OF NEGLECTING ORIGINAL ORDER

A NAIVE, YOUNG ARCHIVIST FROM FT. LAUDER,

ARRANGED RECORDS IN HIS OWN PAINSTAKING AND TEDIOUS ORDER.

FORTY YEARS LATER, HE HAD MADE SUCH A MESS,

HE DECIDED ABRUPTLY (PERHAPS IT WAS BEST),

TO RETIRE FAR SOUTH OF THE BORDER.

LIKE A NEWSPAPER HEADLINE, A GOOD DESCRIPTION TELLS CERTAIN VITAL FACTS...

SUCH AS:

1. THE ORIGIN OF RECORDS.
2. THE TYPE OF RECORDS.
3. THE SUBJECT OF RECORDS.
4. THE DATE OF RECORDS.
5. THE VOLUME OF RECORDS.

LET'S EXAMINE EACH OF THESE BITS OF INFORMATION.

ORIGIN   TYPE
SUBJECT   DATE
     VOLUME

1. ORIGIN OF RECORDS REFLECTS THE OFFICIAL, COMMITTEE, OR OTHER SOURCE WHICH CREATED OR COLLECTED THE SERIES.

2. TYPE REFERS TO THE GENERAL FORMAT OF THE INFORMATION.

AMONG THE MANY TYPES OF RECORDS IN AN ARCHIVES ARE:

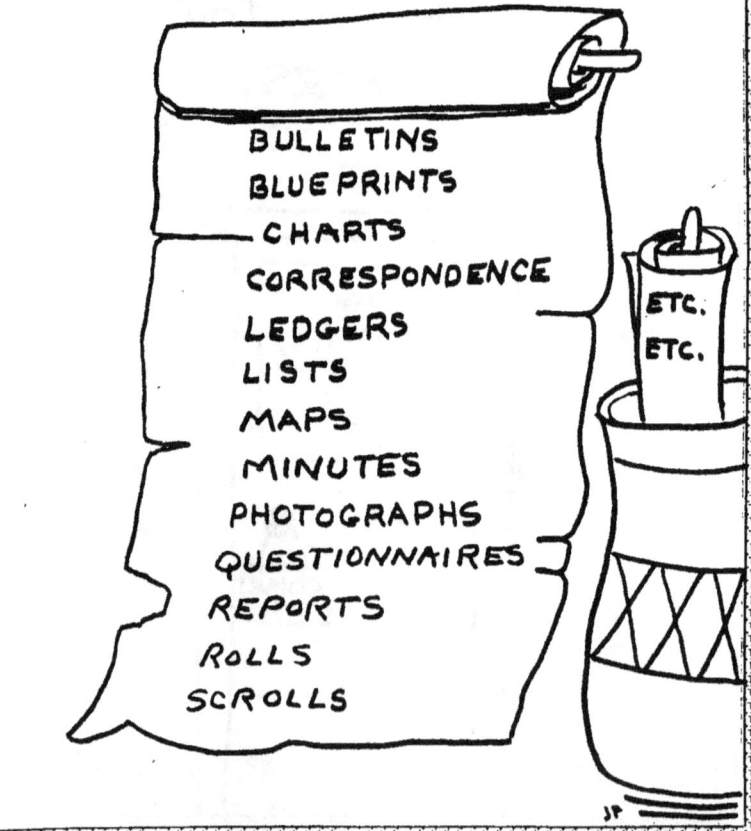

- BULLETINS
- BLUEPRINTS
- CHARTS
- CORRESPONDENCE
- LEDGERS
- LISTS
- MAPS
- MINUTES
- PHOTOGRAPHS
- QUESTIONNAIRES
- REPORTS
- ROLLS
- SCROLLS
- ETC. ETC.

3. THE SUBJECT OF RECORDS WILL BE DIVERSE.

YOU MAY LOCATE HISTORICAL DOCUMENTS ABOUT:

Baptisms and Budgets,

Elections and Evangelism,

Music and Missions,

Sermons and Schools,

Marriages and Mortgages.

4. DATE OF RECORDS.

WHEN DATING SERIES, INDICATE THE INCLUSIVE PERIOD COVERED BEGINNING WITH THE EARLIEST INFORMATION.

EXAMPLE: 1933 - 1956
HOWEVER, A GAP EXISTS IN THE RECORDS FROM 1940 TO 1945.

WRITE: 1933-40; 1946-56.

5. VOLUME OF A RECORD SERIES IS STATED IN FEET, INCHES, OR NUMBER OF BOUND VOLUMES.

AN ARCHIVES BOX IS 5" WIDE.

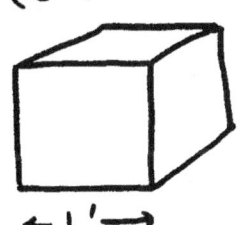
A STANDARD CARTON IS 1 FT. WIDE.

A BOUND VOLUME IS ABBREVIATED B.V.

THESE FIVE BITS OF INFORMATION CAN BE STATED IN A SHORT TITLE.

EXAMPLES:

ORIGIN — TYPE

Pastor Ben Ray's Correspondence relating to Baptisms. 1962 - 1977.   4 ft.

SUBJECT — DATE — VOLUME

ORIGIN — SUBJECT — TYPE — DATE

Church Membership Lists. 1963 - present.
5 B.V. 5 in.

VOLUME

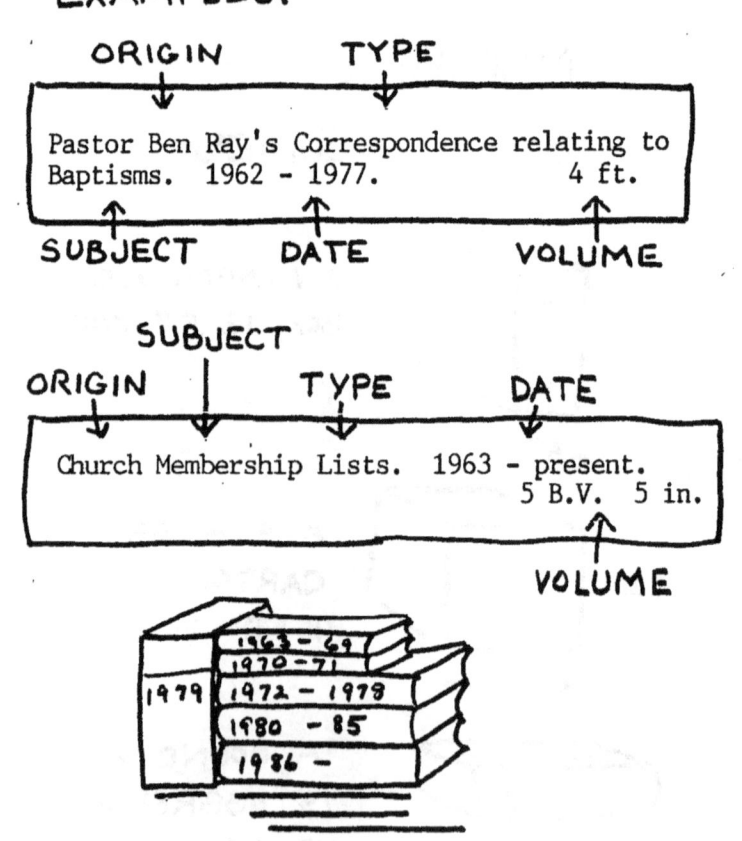

ADDITIONAL INFORMATION ABOUT A SERIES IS INCLUDED IN A

DESCRIPTIVE PARAGRAPH

WHICH MAY INDICATE
- HOW FILES ARE ARRANGED;
- NOTED PERSONS OR EVENTS;
- RELATED RECORDS AVAILABLE;
- OR OTHER FACTS.

EXAMPLE:

Church's 100th Anniversary Guestbook.
Oct. 10, 1990.   1 B.V.

A volume containing handwritten greetings and signatures of persons attending the 100th anniversary of First Church, Norman, Oklahoma. Among the signatures are those of Ruth Gramm, Norman Pinchott Peal, John Wessle, and Philip B. Rooks. Related records, including the anniversary sermon by Bill E. Step may be found in entries 61 through 69.

WHILE THE ARCHIVES STAFF IS ARRANGING AND DESCRIBING RECORDS, THEY WILL FIND PREPRINTED INVENTORY CARDS TO BE HELPFUL.

```
                                    ENTRY #_____
SUBJECT: _____
ORIGIN: _____ DATES: _____
TYPE: _____ VOL: _____
ADDITIONAL INFORMATION: _____
_____
_____
```

OH YES! AN ENTRY NUMBER ASSIGNED TO EACH SERIES DESCRIPTION, AND WRITTEN ON THE RECORD (IN PENCIL OR CHALK), AVOIDS BACKTRACKING AND CONFUSION.

AFTER THE RECORDS HAVE BEEN ARRANGED AND A DESCRIPTION HAS BEEN WRITTEN FOR EACH SERIES, THE INFORMATION SHOULD BE COMPILED INTO A

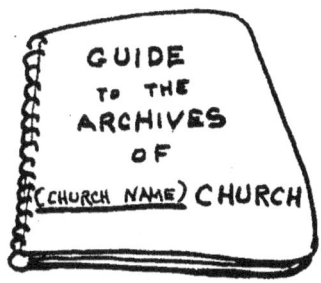

A TYPICAL, COMPLETED GUIDE FOR A CHURCH ARCHIVES WILL INCLUDE THREE SECTIONS.

1. A SHORT HISTORY.

2. AN INDEX.

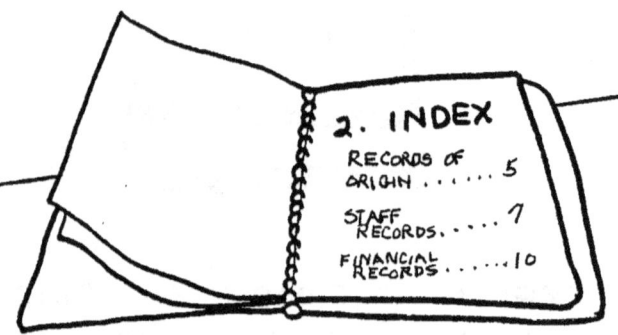

ITEMS IN THE INDEX WILL REFLECT THE **RECORD GROUPS** AND **SUBGROUPS** IN THE ARCHIVAL COLLECTION.

3. SERIES DESCRIPTIONS.

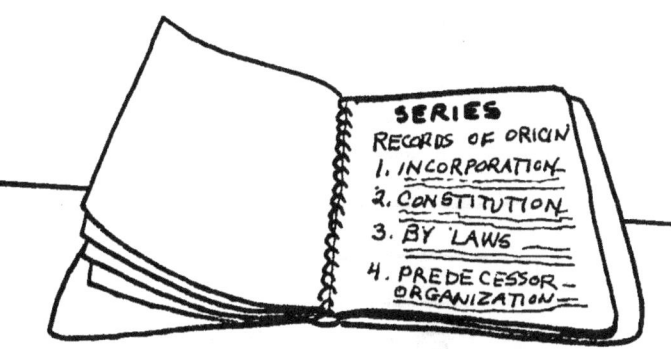

THE **GUIDE** TO **ARCHIVES** WILL BE THE PRIMARY RESEARCH AID IN THE CHURCH ARCHIVES.

- ✔ KEEP THE MASTER COPY IN ARCHIVES BOX 1.

- ✔ MAKE COPIES AVAILABLE TO RESEACHERS.

REVIEW 4

THIS CHAPTER CONTAINS THE BASIC INSTRUCTIONS FOR BUILDING AN ARCHIVES. PLEASE REVIEW CAREFULLY.

1. THE FOUR LEVELS OF ARRANGEMENT ARE:

   _____
   _____
   _____
   _____

   REREAD PAGES 86 TO 99 FOR ANSWERS.

2. FIVE INFORMATION PARTS OF A TITLE ARE:

   _____, _____, _____, _____, AND _____.

   REREAD PAGES 100 TO 112.

3. THE THREE PARTS OF A GUIDE TO ARCHIVES ARE:

   _____, _____ AND _____.

   REVIEW PAGES 113 TO 115.

Chapter V

HOW CAN ARCHIVAL MATERIALS BE PRESERVED?

HOWEVER, ARCHIVISTS CAN USE A VARIETY OF METHODS TO PREVENT LOSS.

AT THE DOCUMENT LEVEL, ARCHIVISTS MAY:

✓ CLEAN RECORDS,

✓ REMOVE EXTRANEOUS MATERIALS SUCH AS PAPER CLIPS AND RUBBER BANDS,

✓ DEACIDIFY CRUMBLING PAPER, AND

✓ COPY MOLDERING RECORDS ONTO ACID-FREE PAPER.

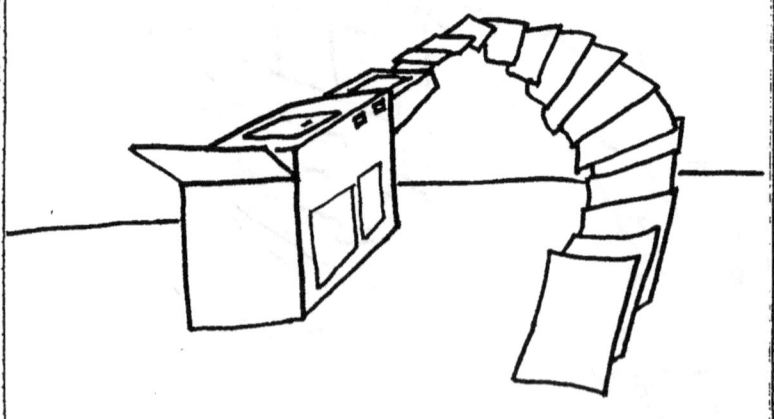

ARCHIVISTS MAY ALSO:

- ✔ FLATTEN FOLDED DOCUMENTS,
- ✔ STORE RECORDS IN ACID-FREE FOLDERS AND BOXES,
- ✔ AVOID EXPOSURE OF RECORDS TO STRONG LIGHT, AND
- ✔ ENCAPSULATE IMPORTANT DOCUMENTS IN CLEAR POLYESTER SLEEVES.

BY PROVIDING AN AIR-CONDITIONED STORAGE SPACE,
A CHURCH CAN PROTECT ITS ARCHIVES FROM

- ✓ HIGH HUMIDITY,
- ✓ FLUCTUATING TEMPERATURES,
- ✓ MOLD, AND
- ✓ CHEMICAL POLLUTION.

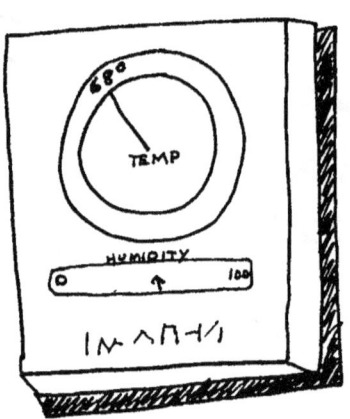

BY PROVIDING A SECURE STORAGE FACILITY, A CHURCH CAN ALSO PROTECT ITS ARCHIVES FROM

- ✓ THEFT,
- ✓ INSECT AND RODENT DAMAGE,
- ✓ FIRE AND FLOOD.

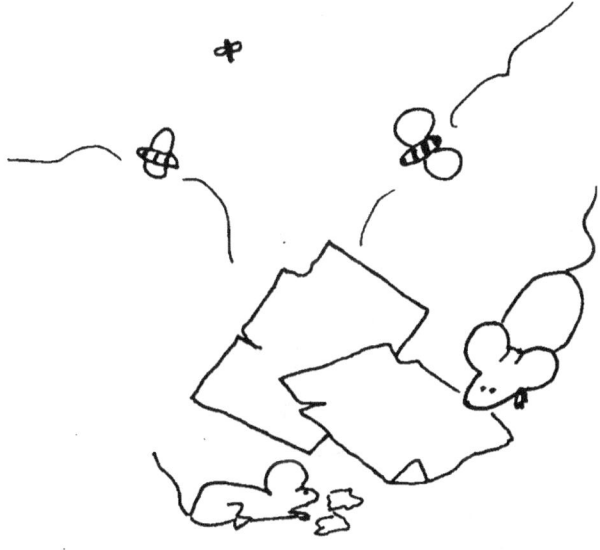

AS A FURTHER PRECAUTION AGAINST CATASTROPHE, CERTAIN IMPORTANT DOCUMENTS SHOULD BE

MICROFILMED.

TO BE USEFUL,
MICROFILMED RECORDS MUST
BE ADEQUATELY ARRANGED
ARRANGED
AND
IDENTIFIED.

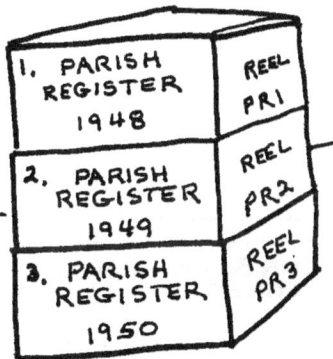

THE COMPANY OR INSTITUTION
WHICH MICROFILMS YOUR RECORDS
WILL PROBABLY PROVIDE
SPECIFIC INSTRUCTIONS.

IDENTIFY EACH SERIES TO BE FILMED BY PREPARING A CARD WITH THE FOLLOWING INFORMATION:

1. NAME OF CHURCH.
2. LOCATION OF CHURCH.
3. SERIES DESCRIPTION FROM THE <u>GUIDE TO ARCHIVES</u>.

```
SAINT JOHN'S CHURCH
334  4TH STREET     OURAY, COLO.

ANNUAL PARISH REPORTS.   1911 TO
1990.                     2 FT.

REPORTS TO BISHOP INCLUDING
NUMBER OF BAPTISMS, CONFIRMATIONS,
MARRIAGES + BURIALS; A SUMMARY OF
RECEIPTS AND EXPENDITURES; STATE-
MENT OF PROPERTY. FROM 1951
ONWARD REPORTS ARE ON PRINTED.
```

ASK THE FILMING AGENCY TO PROVIDE THE CHURCH WITH TWO COPIES OF THE MICROFILM.

STORE ONE COPY IN A FIREPROOF VAULT.

USE THE SECOND COPY FOR REFERENCE IN THE ARCHIVES.

LET'S REVIEW
PRESERVATION IN ARCHIVES.

Match the cartoons below with the statements which describe ways archivists can prevent losses in archives.

1. Store in temperature- and humidity controlled space.

2. Avoid exposure of records to strong light.

3. Copy damaged records on to acid-free paper.

4. Prevent damage by rodents and insects.

5. Protect archives from fire and water.

6. Microfilm documents.

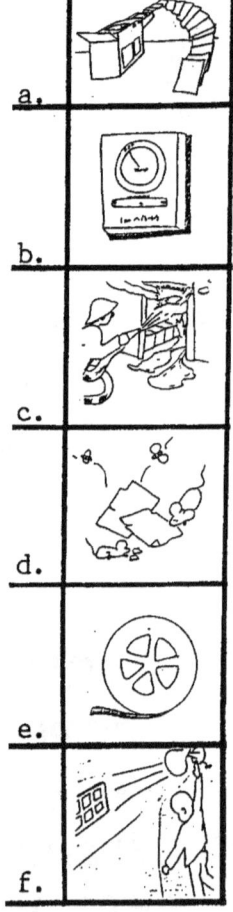

a.

b.

c.

d.

e.

f.

ANSWERS:
1. b; 2. f; 3. a; 4. d; 5. c; 6. e.

Chapter VI

HOW CAN CHURCHES USE ARCHIVES?

AS WE NOTED IN CHAPTER ONE, A CHURCH MAY USE ITEMS FROM ITS ARCHIVES

FOR ANNIVERSARY CELEBRATIONS,

OR FOR THE WRITING OF CHURCH HISTORY.

ARCHIVAL DOCUMENTS MAY ALSO BE USED IN

NEW MEMBER ORIENTATION,

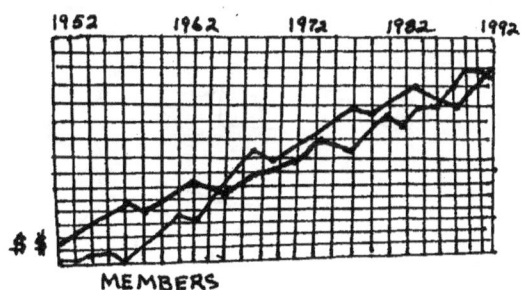

FUND-RAISING ACTIVITIES,

AND OTHER OCCASIONS.

UNFORTUNATELY,
CARELESS USE
CAN CAUSE GREAT LOSS
IN ARCHIVES.

THESE RULES SHOULD ESTABLISH:

1. WHO MAY USE RECORDS.

USUALLY, RECORDS ARE EQUALLY AVAILABLE TO ALL ADULTS.

A CHURCH SHOULD REQUIRE USERS TO COMPLETE A RESEARCHER'S IDENTIFICATION CARD.

```
                         DATE _____
  NAME: _____
  ADDRESS: _____
           _____

  PHONE: _____

  REASON FOR REQUEST: _____
  _____
  _____

  RECORDS NEEDED: _____
  _____
```

2. WHEN AND WHERE ARCHIVES MAY BE STUDIED.

MOST CHURCH ARCHIVES WILL BE AVAILABLE BY APPOINTMENT ONLY. THE CHURCH LIBRARY OR A CHURCH OFFICE MAY BE A CONVENIENT, SECURE PLACE FOR STUDY.

THE ARCHIVES STAFF MUST MAKE SURE THAT THE RECORDS ARE RETURNED TO THEIR PROPER LOCATION AFTER EACH USE.

3. PROCEDURES FOR LOANING RECORDS.

WHEN A DOCUMENT IS LOANED FOR USE INSIDE THE CHURCH BUILDING, A CHARGEOUT CARD MUST BE COMPLETED IN DUPLICATE.

```
DATE: _____
ORGANIZATION: _____
RESPONSIBLE INDIVIDUAL: _____
LOCATION WHERE RECORD WILL BE
DISPLAYED/USED: _____
```

ONE COPY OF THE CARD WILL BE PLACED IN A CHARGEOUT BOX.

THE OTHER COPY IS PLACED IN THE LOCATION WHERE THE RECORD WAS REMOVED.

OUTSIDE LOANS SHOULD BE SUBJECT TO THESE CONDITIONS:

1. ARCHIVAL MATERIALS ARE LOANED ONLY TO OTHER INSTITUTIONS, NEVER TO INDIVIDUALS.

2. THE OFFICIAL OF A BORROWING INSTITUTION SHALL PROVIDE A RECEIPT FOR THE RECORDS AND SHALL BE RESPONSIBLE FOR THEIR PROMPT RETURN.

3. FRAGILE RECORDS WHICH MAY BE ENDANGERED BY HANDLING ARE NOT LOANED.

4. DOCUMENTS OF EXCEPTIONAL INTRINSIC VALUE ARE NOT LOANED.

4. GUIDELINES FOR MAKING COPIES OF DOCUMENTS, TAPES, OR PHOTOGRAPHS.

AND CURRENT COPYING DEVICES ARE A BOON TO ARCHIVISTS <u>AND</u> RESEARCHERS.

A. PROVIDE COPIES TO RESEARCHERS AT COST.

B. AVOID DAMAGE TO RECORDS WHILE MAKING COPIES.

5. COSTS
FOR SERVICES.

MICROFILM $5.00 PER ROLL

PHOTOCOPIES 10¢ EACH

DESCRIPTIONS OF RECORDS FREE

POSTAGE AND INSURANCE AT COSTS

BOOK SUMMARY

Chapter I

Why Do Churches Need Archives?

"An Archives helps a church preserve its heritage."

"Excuse me. That sounds like a wonderful reason to have an archives. But, I'm not really sure what an archives is."

"You've raised a good point.

Archives are the official, non-current records of a church which have been preserved for future use."

"Official? I suppose you mean records which are made by church officers or in a church office. But, non-current? Does that mean like things you would find in a museum?"

"No. A museum is a collection of artifacts. An archives is a body of historical documents."

"Documents? Such as a library?"

"Well, almost. But a library is a collection of published materials. An archives contains one-of-a-kind records, such as the minutes of a church business meeting."

"So, you are saying that

Archives are the official, non-current records of a church which have been preserved for future use."

"Exactly! Now let's think about why churches need archives."

"An Archives provides a clear picture of a church's past--undistorted by bias, prejudice, or forgetfulness. Because of this, archives have been called the primary building blocks of history. Church archives also join together to form an accurate account of denominational history. An archives helps a church to remember its original purpose. Patrick Henry said, "I have but one lamp to light the future and that is the lamp of the past."

"Oh, those ideas are quite inspiring! But, what are the practical reasons for having a church archives?"

"Practical reasons? OK. An archives preserves legal and historical documents, such as blueprints, deeds, charters, surveys, etc. An archives also preserves personal records which reflect family history, such as baptismal, marriage, and death records. An archives demonstrates the influence of the church in the community. Archives facilitate present activities by helping the church examine the past in order to plan future activities. Thus, they may repeat successful activities, as well as avoid mistakes of earlier years. Anniversaries and other celebrations are enhanced by a display of archival materials. And last, an archives makes the writing of a church history more complete and more accurate.

Chapter II

How Can Churches Begin Archives?

Beginning an archives is not difficult. Inertia is the main problem. These four procedures will help you get started:

1. Enlist an archivist and staff.
2. Locate the church's historical records.
3. Designate a storage area.
4. Purchase supplies.

Let's examine each operation.

1. Enlist an archivist and staff. Some churches call this a historical committee. Some qualifications for this task are: A love of history, a sense of order, and the ability to complete a task.

2. Locate historical records. Ask the pastor to help publicize the search. Secretaries may have valuable suggestions. The building custodian could help locate a treasure trove. Former church officers may bring outdated records from home. Advertize in various ways. Use the church bulletin too. Set a deadline for collection of records.

3. Designate a storage space--near a process and research area, temperature and humidity controlled, if possible. Avoid storage areas subject to flooding, in hot or cold attics, in a coffee break room, or near a heat source.

4. Purchase supplies: acid-free file folders, archives boxes, cubic-foot cartons, baked-enamel file cabinets, chalk, marking pens, and labels.

Chapter III

Which Records Should Be Preserved?

The archives committee has now collected many historical records. You ask, "Must we keep everything?" No, almost all church records need winnowing to separate the wheat from the chaff. Consider this, church records are created to fill an administrative need, but archives must have value beyond the purpose for which they were created.

To help determine the worth of a record, ask these questions: What is the record's legal value? artistic value? historical value? family value? denominational value? emotional value? administrative value? Ask, If this document were dated 100 years earlier, would I find it more interesting, informative, worthwhile? Ask, Is the document well preserved? If records are illegible, mildewed, damaged by rodents or insects, they may not be worth keeping.

The key to significant quality in archives is records management. This means a church should adequately document its actions. Records management also means that a church should decide which records to retain.

Selection of records for archives may be done by chance. But a written selection guide is a more reliable method! So develop a written records selection guide appropriate for your church and ask your church to approve. (A sample records selection guide is included at the end of Chapter III.) Records which provide a good picture of a church's history are staff correspondence, minutes of church business meetings, weekly bulletins, annual statistical reports, and photographs identified by date, place, person, and activity.

Selection of records for church archives involves disposal as well as preservation of records. Therefore, separation of records should be done by more than one person.

Chapter IV

How Should Archival Materials be Organized?

The difference between a pile of broken glass and a stained glass window is arrangement. In the same manner, the difference between a roomful of dusty church records and an archives is arrangement. Records must not only be arranged in an orderly manner, they must also be described to aid a researcher to determine what records are available. Someone may ask, "Who was the pastor in 1957?" Or, "Does the education building have plumbing for an extra kitchen?" Or, "What was the church budget in 1933?" Efficient arrangement and description of records pave the way to answer such questions. As the archivists arrange records, they can also make notes for use in writing descriptions.

First, let's talk about arrangement. Church records will probably need to be arranged on several levels.

1. Record group. 2. Sub-group. 3. Series. 4. File units.

1. Record group. A church archives should be organized by record groups. Each records group will represent the administrative unit which originally made or accumulated the records. The French first used record groups after the revolution when they took custody of the royal records. They called it <u>respect des fonds</u>. This means that records from one source must not be mingled with records from another source.

2. Sub group. For more definitive organization, record groups may be divided into sub groups. (Smaller groups may not need to be subdivided.) Church school records could be divided into nursery, children, youth, adult, new members, and vacation Bible school records. Another example: Church published materials might be

divided into sub groups of bulletins, news letters, membership directories, programs for special events, church histories, sermons, and advertisements.

3. Series. The basic unit of an archival collection is a series. A series is a group of records related by subject, activity, or form.

4. File units. Each series of records may be arranged internally by file units. Common arrangement patterns are chronological, alphabetical, geographical, and numerical.

If possible, the original order of records should be preserved. This means the archivist will arrange documents in the same order that the creator of the records arranged. But, if the records are in complete disarray, the archivist may impose a system of organization to aid retrieval. In this case, the simplest system is the best system.

Now, let's talk about description. The purpose of description is to present an accurate picture of each series within the archives. Like a newspaper headline, a good description tells certain vital facts, such as 1. the origin of the records, 2. the type of records, 3. the subject of the records, 4. the date of the records, and 5. the volume of the records. Let's examine each of these bits of information.

1. Origin of records reflects the official, committee, or other source which created or collected the record series. 2. Type refers to the general format of the information. Among the many types of records in an archives are bulletins, blueprints, charts, correspondence, ledgers, lists, maps, minutes, photographs, questionnaires, reports, rolls,

scrolls, and so forth. 3. The <u>subject</u> of records will be diverse. You may locate historical documents about baptisms and budgets, elections and evangelism, music and missions, sermons and schools, marriages and mortgages. 4. <u>Date</u> of records. When dating series, indicate the inclusive period covered, beginning with earliest information. Example: 1933-1956. However, a gap exists in the records from 1940-1945. Write: 1933-40: 1946-56. 5. <u>Volume</u> of a record series is stated in feet, inches, or number of bound volumes. An archives box is 5" wide. A standard carton is 1 ft. wide. A bound volume is abbreviated B.V.

These five bits of information can be stated in a short title. Example: Pastor Ben Ray's (origin) Correspondence (type) relating to Baptisms (subject). 1962-1977 (date). 4 ft. (volume).

Additional information about a series is included in a descriptive paragraph which may indicate how files are arranged, noted person or events, related records available, or other facts. Example:

Church's 100th Anniversary Guestbook. Oct. 10-1990. One B. V.

A volume containing handwritten greetings and signatures of persons attending the 100th anniversary of First Church, Norman, Oklahoma. Among the signatures are those of Ruth Gramm, Norman Pinchott Peal, John Wessle, and Philip B. Rooks. Related records including the anniversary sermon by Wm. Step may be found in entries 61 thru 69.

While the archives staff is arranging and describing records, they will find preprinted inventory cards helpful. An entry number assigned to each series description and written on the record in pencil or chalk, avoids backtracking and confusion.

After the records have been arranged and a description has been written for each series, the information should be compiled into a <u>Guide to the Archives of (name) Church.</u> A typical guide will include three sections: 1. A short history, 2. An index to series, and 3. Series descriptions. <u>The Guide to Archives</u> will be the primary research aid in the church archives. Keep the master copy in Archives box 1. Make copies available to researchers.

Chapter V

How Can Archival Materials be Preserved?

Ancient archivists had an easy job. Their records were durable. Alas, modern archival records are perishable! Paper crumbles and inks fade. Fire, water, and a host of other enemies cause losses in archives. However, archivists can use a variety of methods to prevent loss. At the document level, archivists may clean records; remove extraneous materials, such as paper clips and rubber bands; deacidify crumbling paper, and copy moldering records onto acid-free paper. Archivists may also flatten folded documents; store records in acid-free folders and boxes; avoid exposure of records to strong light; and encapsulate important document in clear polyester sleeves.

By providing an air-conditioned storage space, a church can protect archives from high humidity, fluctuating temperature, mold, and chemical pollution. By providing a secure storage facility, a church can also protect its archives from theft, insect and rodent damage, fire and flood.

As a further precaution against catastrophe, certain important documents should be microfilmed. To be useful, microfilmed records must be adequately arranged and identified. The company or institution which microfilms your records will probably provide specific instructions. Identify each series to be filmed by preparing a card with the name of church, location of church, and the series description from <u>The Guide to Archives.</u> Ask the filming agency to provide the church with two copies of the microfilm. Store one copy in a fireproof vault. Use the second copy for reference in the archives.

Chapter VI

How Can Churches Use Archives?

As we noted in Chapter one, a church may use items from its archives for anniversary celebrations, or for the writing of church history. Archival documents may also be used in new member orientation, fund-raising activities, and other occasions. Unfortunately, careless use can cause great loss in archives. Therefore, a church should establish guidelines which will protect its archival materials. These rules should establish:

1. Who may use the records. Usually, records are equally available to all adults. A church should require users to complete a researcher's identification card including date, name, address, phone number, reason for request, and records needed.

2. When and where archives may be studied. Most churches will make archives available by appointment only. The church library or a church office may be a convenient, secure place for study. The archives staff must make sure that the records are returned to their proper location after each use.

3. Procedures for loaning records. When a document is loaned for use inside the building, a chargeout card must be completed in duplicate. One copy of the card will be placed in a chargeout box. The other copy is placed in the location where the record was removed. Outside loans should be subject to these conditions: 1. Archival materials are loaned only to other institutions, never to individuals. 2. The official of a borrowing institution shall provide a receipt for the records and shall be responsible for their prompt return. 3. Fragile records which may be endangered by handling are not loaned. 4. Documents of exceptional intrinsic value are not loaned.

4. Guidelines for making copies of documents, tapes, or photographs.

5. Costs for services.

www.ingramcontent.com/pod-product-compliance
Lightning Source LLC
Chambersburg PA
CBHW072145160426
43197CB00012B/2255